W9-BXU-941

JAGUARS

by Vicky Franchino

Children's Press®

An Imprint of Scholastic Inc.
New York Toronto London Auckland Sydney
Mexico City New Delhi Hong Kong
Danbury, Connecticut

Content Consultant
Dr. Stephen S. Ditchkoff
Professor of Wildlife Sciences
Auburn University
Auburn, Alabama

Library of Congress Cataloging-in-Publication Data
Franchino, Vicky.
 Jaguars / by Vicky Franchino.
 pages cm—(Nature's children)
 Includes bibliographical references and index.
 ISBN 978-0-531-23360-3 (lib. bdg.) —
 ISBN 978-0-531-25158-4 (pbk.)
 1. Jaguar—Juvenile literature. I. Title.
 QL737.C23F729 2013
 599.75′5—dc23   2013000093

Printed in China 62
SCHOLASTIC, CHILDREN'S PRESS, and associated logos are
trademarks and/or registered trademarks of Scholastic Inc.

1 2 3 4 5 6 7 8 9 10 R 23 22 21 20 19 18 17 16 15 14

Jaguars

Class	Mammalia
Order	Carnivora
Family	Felidae
Genus	*Panthera*
Species	*Panthera onca*
World distribution	North America, Central America, South America
Habitats	Rain forests, grasslands, swamp areas, forests, woodlands, and sometimes desert areas
Distinctive physical characteristics	Typically golden or reddish-brown fur with black rosette markings; body is stockier than other big cats; very large head; extremely strong jaws and sharp teeth that can pierce shells and bones
Habits	Lives on its own except when caring for cubs or mating; tends to hunt at dusk or dawn; stalks and pounces on prey; hunts animals on land, in water, and in trees
Diet	Entirely carnivorous; eats both large and small animals, including reptiles; favorite prey includes deer, capybaras (large rodents), and caimans (members of the crocodile family)

JAGUARS

Contents

CHAPTER 1

Silent and Strong

As the sun creeps over the horizon, a young deer stops at the edge of a swiftly flowing river deep in the heart of the Amazon rain forest. Plants and a refreshing drink are nearby. It is time for breakfast! Unfortunately for the deer, another animal is also ready for its first meal of the day. In the forest's dark underbrush, a patient jaguar waits. With barely a sound, it leaps from its hiding place.

The jaguar is one of the only big cats in the Western Hemisphere, which includes North, Central, and South America. The jaguar is a strong and cunning animal that has just one **predator**: humans. Its name comes from *yaguara*, a Native American word that means "he who kills with one leap." This **carnivore** will eat virtually any animal that lives on land, in water, or even in the trees.

Jaguars rely on plant growth to help them stay hidden as they silently stalk their prey.

A Big Cat

The jaguar is the third-largest member of the cat family. Only the tiger and the lion are bigger. The average male jaguar weighs between 70 and 249 pounds (32 and 113 kilograms). Females are usually about 10 to 20 percent smaller. The heaviest jaguar ever recorded weighed nearly 350 pounds (159 kg). Jaguars are usually between 4 and 7 feet (1.2 and 2.1 meters) long, with a tail that is almost half the length of the body. They are usually between 27 and 30 inches (69 and 76 centimeters) tall at the shoulder. The jaguar has a very large head compared to the rest of its body.

Adult male
6 ft. (1.8 m)

Jaguar
30 in. tall (76 cm)

7 ft. long (2.1 m)

Jaguars that live in forests are usually smaller than those that live in more open areas.

At Home in Many Places

Although jaguars have occasionally been seen in the southwestern areas of the United States and in Mexico, most live in Central and South America.

Jaguars can live in many different **habitats**, including grasslands and rain forests. They are at home on the ground or in the trees. A smaller jaguar may climb into a tree to sleep or to lie in wait for an animal to walk by. During floods, jaguars sometimes climb into the trees until the water goes down. For food they can rely on the birds, monkeys, and other creatures that live there.

Unlike most cats, jaguars like the water and are strong swimmers. On a hot day, a nearby river or lake becomes a giant swimming pool where the jaguar can take a refreshing dip. The water is also a source of food. The jaguar will reach right into the water and grab a fish to eat!

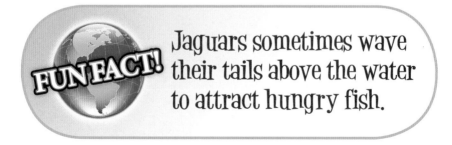

FUN FACT! Jaguars sometimes wave their tails above the water to attract hungry fish.

Experts believe that jaguars swim not only to chase prey but also to bathe.

CHAPTER 2

Hidden Hunter

The jaguar's body is designed for stalking and hunting. Jaguars have padded feet, which help them surprise their victims. The jaguar is almost silent as it sneaks up on its target.

Most jaguars have a fur coat that is deep gold or reddish brown. Their bodies are covered with markings. A jaguar's head and legs are covered with black dots, and circular shapes called rosettes are spread across its side and back. This combination of light and dark coloring provides **camouflage** for the jaguar and lets it disappear into its surroundings.

Some jaguars have high levels of **pigment**. This causes their fur to turn very dark instead of gold or brown. At first glance, these jaguars might not appear to have markings, but a closer look shows that they do. White jaguars have also been seen, but they are very rare.

Around 6 percent of all jaguars have dark fur.
They tend to live in areas with heavier forest cover.

Time to Eat!

Jaguars are not picky eaters. They have been known to eat more than 80 kinds of animals. Although they will eat almost any creature they can find, they do have favorite meals. These include deer, a large rodent called a capybara, and a member of the alligator family called a caiman. A jaguar can kill animals that are very large, including animals that are bigger than it is!

Although a jaguar can chase its prey for short distances, it usually waits quietly and relies on the element of surprise to attack. Extremely strong jaw muscles and sharp teeth help the jaguar kill its prey. While many cats kill prey by crushing the animal's throat, jaguars can bite through its skull. A jaguar's long, sharp teeth and tough jaws can even break through the shell of a turtle!

The jaguar's tongue is covered with bumps called papillae. The papillae have two jobs. They help the jaguar scrape meat off bones, and they act like little cups when the jaguar gets a drink.

Caimans are dangerous hunters, but they are no match for the mighty jaguar.

Senses for Survival

Jaguars usually decide when to sleep based on the habits of their prey. They tend to be crepuscular, which means they are most active around dawn and dusk.

Like all big cats, jaguars can see very well in the dark. They have a special reflective layer of tissue in the back of their eyes called tapetum lucidum. This tissue is behind the retina. The retina processes the images that come into the eye and sends information to the brain. When light comes into the eye, the tapetum lucidum acts like a giant mirror and reflects the light back. This creates almost twice as much light in the retina and makes it easier for a jaguar to see at night.

The jaguar's world is filled with noises and scents. Its keen hearing and sense of smell help it sort out which sounds and scents mean that dinner is hiding nearby!

The pupils at the center of a jaguar's eyes get larger in the dark to let in more light and shrink in bright light to keep the cat from being blinded.

Cat Communication

Smells help a jaguar talk to other jaguars. A jaguar will use stinky urine and droppings to mark its **territory**. It will also rub its body against trees and bushes. Other jaguars recognize these smells and know that an area has already been claimed. Markings on trees are another way to communicate. A jaguar will make deep scratches in the bark of a tree to mark its territory. Scratching a tree also helps a jaguar keep its claws sharp.

Female jaguars use smells to get a male's attention. When a female jaguar wants to **mate**, the smell of her urine is one way she will let the male jaguar know.

Like all cats, the jaguar uses its voice. A roar says, "That's mine" or "Go away." Jaguars also growl, grunt, and snarl to get their messages across.

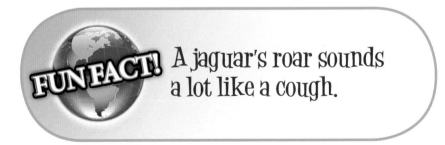

FUN FACT! A jaguar's roar sounds a lot like a cough.

Just as pet cats scratch at posts and toys, jaguars must scratch trees to keep their claws sharp and strong.

CHAPTER 3

Alone but Not Lonely

Adult male jaguars spend nearly all of their time alone. They hunt alone. They eat and sleep alone. They live in a territory that can range up to 30 square miles (78 square kilometers). If there isn't enough to eat, a jaguar might have to expand its territory.

The only time an adult male jaguar looks for company is when it is time to mate. If two males are interested in the same female, one will usually roar to scare the other off. It is very unusual for jaguars to fight over a female.

Once mating is over, the male jaguar goes back to its solitary life. It does not help the female care for the cubs when they're born. In fact, a female jaguar will chase a father away from his cubs out of fear that he might eat them!

Roaring jaguars look ferocious even when they are playing.

Family Matters

It takes between 95 and 110 days after mating for a female jaguar to give birth. When a female jaguar knows that her babies are about to be born, she looks for a safe place to give birth. A cave, a space under a bush, or dense tree roots can all provide protection for her babies.

A jaguar litter can have between one and four cubs. Two is the most common number. Jaguar cubs are long and lean when they're born. They usually weigh between 1.5 and 2 pounds (0.7 and 0.9 kg) and are about 16 inches (41 cm) long. Newborn jaguars have spots and fur that are brownish and blotchy looking. Jaguars are blind at birth and quite helpless. They depend entirely on their mother for survival.

Newborn jaguars nurse from their mother for the first months of their lives. When they are about six months old, they start to join their mother as she hunts for food. They watch her carefully to learn how to hunt for themselves.

Jaguar cubs are often born with blue eyes, but the eyes generally darken to gold with time.

Growing Up

Jaguar cubs stay with their mother for protection and food until they are between one and two years old. Then the young jaguars need to find territory of their own. A male will move far away, but a young female's territory might overlap with her mother's. Males will sometimes let a female share some portion of their territory, but they will not allow males to hunt nearby.

Female and male jaguars reach maturity at different ages. A female is ready to have cubs of her own when she is about one to two years old. A male jaguar doesn't mate for the first time until it is three or four years old.

In the wild, jaguars usually live between 12 and 15 years. In captivity, some have been known to survive for more than 20 years.

Jaguar mothers show affection for their cubs by licking them.

The Cat Family

Jaguars are members of the cat, or Felidae, family. Cats are believed to have first appeared around 60 million years ago. Scientists believe that the *Panthera* **genus**—which also includes tigers, lions, and leopards—broke off from the larger cat family sometime between 4.3 million and 3.8 million years ago. Jaguars began to appear later, probably between 3.6 million and 2.5 million years ago.

Ancestors of today's jaguar once lived in Europe and Asia. They traveled to North America over the Bering land bridge, which used to connect Alaska and Asia. After this bridge disappeared under water about 10,000 years ago, jaguars had no way to travel between these continents. They eventually died out in Europe and Asia.

Jaguar **fossils** have been found throughout North America in places such as Tennessee, Texas, and the La Brea Tar Pits in California. The jaguar eventually began to move south into Central and South America, where it lives today.

Fossils show that ancient jaguar relatives were larger than the jaguars living today.

Size Matters

For a long time, scientists believed there were a number of different **subspecies** of jaguars. As scientists have learned more about **genes**, they have been able to compare different jaguars. In the year 2000, scientists officially announced that there is only one kind of jaguar.

One reason that they originally thought there must be different types was because jaguars come in a variety of sizes. Scientists have now decided that the size differences are because of the jaguar's food supply. Jaguars that live in areas with large prey and abundant food often grow to be larger than jaguars that live in areas with more limited food. Generally speaking, there is a divide between northern and southern countries. Jaguars that live in Mexico and Costa Rica are usually smaller than those in Brazil and Argentina.

Jaguars from Costa Rica are smaller than most of their relatives.

Lions and Tigers

The jaguar is closely related to the two biggest members of the cat family—the lion and the tiger. These ferocious beasts are carnivores and have almost no predators except for humans. Unlike most cats, tigers, lions, and jaguars are all good swimmers.

Nearly all lions live in Africa, though some can be found in India. Unlike jaguars, lions live in large groups that work together to hunt, defend their territory, and protect their young. Lions are much bigger than jaguars. On average, a male lion weighs between 370 and 500 pounds (168 and 227 kg).

Tigers live in India, China, Russia, and Southeast Asia. These huge animals can weigh almost 700 pounds (318 kg). Like jaguars, adult male tigers are solitary and never form a family unit. They eat a variety of food, including turtles.

A group of lions is called a pride.

Jaguar or Leopard?

It can be hard to tell the difference between a leopard and a jaguar. After all, they usually both have golden fur—though they can sometimes have black or white fur, too—and they both have rosettes.

There are some important differences that can be used to tell the two animals apart. One is the appearance of their rosettes. A jaguar's rosettes have a broken edge, and there are typically lines or circles inside them. Leopards' rosettes are smaller, closer together, and don't have any markings inside them.

Jaguars also have bigger heads than leopards and are stockier in appearance. Their tails are shorter and thicker. The leopard looks leaner and more graceful.

The most important difference is where they live. Leopards are found on the continents of Africa and Asia, while jaguars are found only in the Americas.

Like jaguars, leopards are powerful hunters. They prey on animals such as deer, wild dogs, and apes.

CHAPTER 5

Jaguars at Risk

There are only about 15,000 jaguars left in the world. They are not yet considered **endangered**, but there are reasons to be concerned about them. Jaguars can currently be found in 18 countries, but they have disappeared from almost half of the areas where they used to live. Jaguars are now extinct in the countries of El Salvador and Uruguay.

There are many reasons why the jaguar population is shrinking. One is hunting. Some people hunt jaguars for their beautiful fur. In the 1960s and 1970s, nearly 18,000 jaguars a year were killed for their coats. In 1973, an international group called the Convention on International Trade in Endangered Species passed a law that made it illegal to sell furs or body parts of endangered animals. This has helped, but illegal hunting still happens, and some countries do not recognize the law.

Even though it is illegal, people often pay large amounts of money for jaguar skins.

A Safe Place to Live

Today, the jaguar's biggest problem is loss of habitat. As more wild lands are used for farming or developed to build roads, homes, and businesses, there are fewer places for the jaguar to live. There are also fewer places for its prey to live. As wild animals disappear, jaguars go in search of other food. Many times they attack livestock. Angry farmers trap or kill the jaguars to protect their animals.

Conservation groups are working to find ways to defend the jaguar while still allowing the people of South and Central America to use the land to earn a living. One way is by creating safe places for jaguars to live. For example, the Cockscomb Basin Wildlife Sanctuary was opened in the country of Belize in 1990. It was the first preserve built for jaguars.

Jaguars need plenty of wild prey, such as this bare-faced curassow, to keep from going hungry.

The Jaguar Corridor

Scientists have another way to protect jaguars. Instead of keeping them in certain areas, scientists are creating a jaguar corridor. This corridor is based on the natural paths that jaguars travel, ranging from Mexico to Argentina. This corridor is better than a reserve because it connects jaguars from different areas instead of blocking them off from the rest of the world.

Scientists work with governments and builders to stop development and farming on the paths. They also teach the people in these areas not to shoot the jaguars.

It is not always easy to find the jaguar path. Researchers sometimes track jaguars with camera traps. Cameras are set up on a tree or bush. When jaguars walk past it, they cross a beam of light and the camera takes their picture. These photos help scientists have a better idea of how many jaguars are in an area and how they move about their territory.

Camera traps at hidden locations can take photos of jaguars that would be impossible for live photographers to capture.

Coexisting with Jaguars

Another project is in the Pantanal region. This is a wetland area in Brazil, Bolivia, and Paraguay. It is home to the world's largest population of jaguars, but it has also become a popular place for cattle ranches. The ranchers often shoot the jaguars on sight because they are afraid the cats will kill their cattle.

Conservation groups are trying to find ways for the cattle ranchers and the jaguars to live together in this area. They are working to understand jaguar habits. The more they can learn about jaguars, the easier it will be to find ways for the jaguars and the ranchers to coexist. Scientists hope that the Pantanal study can be a model for other programs.

The survival of the jaguar depends on people working together to guard this incredible cat's habitat. These projects are an important start.

Because jaguars are solitary and secretive, they can be very difficult to study in the wild.

Words to Know

ancestors (AN-ses-turz) — ancient animal species that are related to modern species

camouflage (KAM-uh-flahzh) — a disguise or a natural coloring that allows animals, people, or objects to hide by making them look like their surroundings

captivity (kap-TIV-uh-tee) — the condition of being held or trapped by people

carnivore (KAHR-nuh-vor) — an animal that eats meat

corridor (KOR-i-dur) — a long hall or passage

endangered (en-DAYN-jurd) — at risk of becoming extinct, usually because of human activity

fossils (FAH-suhlz) — bones, shells, or other traces of an animal or plant from long ago, preserved as rock

genes (JEENZ) — one of the parts that make up chromosomes; genes are passed from parents to children and determine how they look and the way they grow

genus (JEE-nuhs) — a group of related plants or animals that is larger than a species but smaller than a family

habitats (HAB-uh-tats) — the places where an animal or a plant is usually found

litter (LIT-ur) — a number of baby animals that are born at the same time to the same mother

livestock (LIVE-stahk) — animals that are kept or raised on a farm or ranch

mate (MATE) — to join together to produce babies

nurse (NURS) — feed a baby milk

pigment (PIG-muhnt) — a substance that gives color to something predator (PRED-uh-tur) — an animal that lives by hunting other animals for food

prey (PRAY) — an animal that's hunted by another animal for food

species (SPEE-sheez) — one of the groups into which animals and plants of the same genus are divided; members of the same species can mate and have offspring

subspecies (SUHB-spee-sheez) — groups of animals that are part of the same species, but are different in some important ways

territory (TER-uh-tor-ee) — area of land claimed by an animal

Habitat Map

NORTH

AMERICA

PACIFIC

OCEAN

ATLANTIC

SOUTH

AMERICA

Jaguar Range